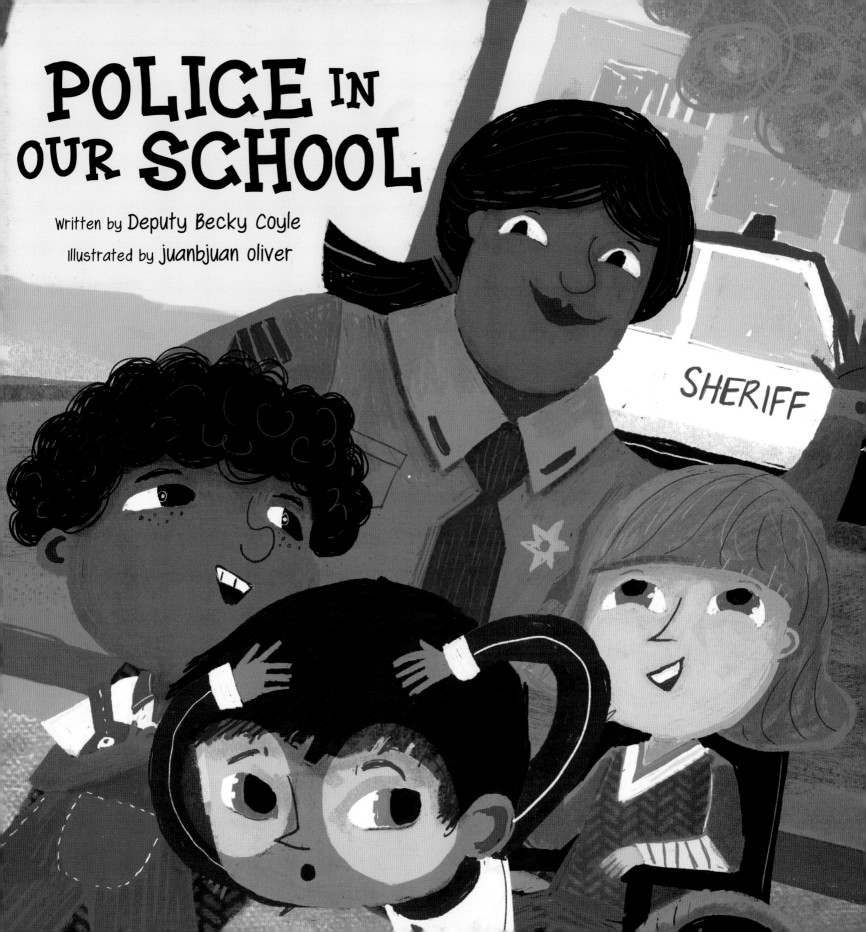

POLICE IN OUR SCHOOL

Written by Deputy Becky Coyle

Illustrated by juanbjuan oliver

SHERIFF

Dedicated to the Williamson County Sheriff's Department SRO Division, Williamson County Schools, and to Kinsley, Dallas, Thea, and Marley Rose.

Special thank you to Mrs. Maggi Margaret Turner, who made this book project possible.

-Becky

Designed by Flowerpot Press
in Franklin, TN.
www.FlowerpotPress.com
Designer: Stephanie Meyers
Editor: Katrine Crow
CHC-1010-0428
ISBN: 978-1-4867-0940-3
Made in China/Fabriqué en Chine

Hi, my name is Becky. I am a deputy sheriff and school resource officer. I love teaching children just like you the importance of being safe while they are playing and learning at school.

Sometimes it is hard to understand why you have to practice drills and follow school rules, but being prepared is an important part of keeping your school safe. Your teachers, school officer, classmates, and even YOU play an important role in ensuring that your school is a place where you can do all of the things that you love to do! By working together and following the rules, we can accomplish so much!

For more information, discussion topics, and activities, visit my website!

www.Cops4Schools.com.

Stay safe,
Deputy Becky Coyle

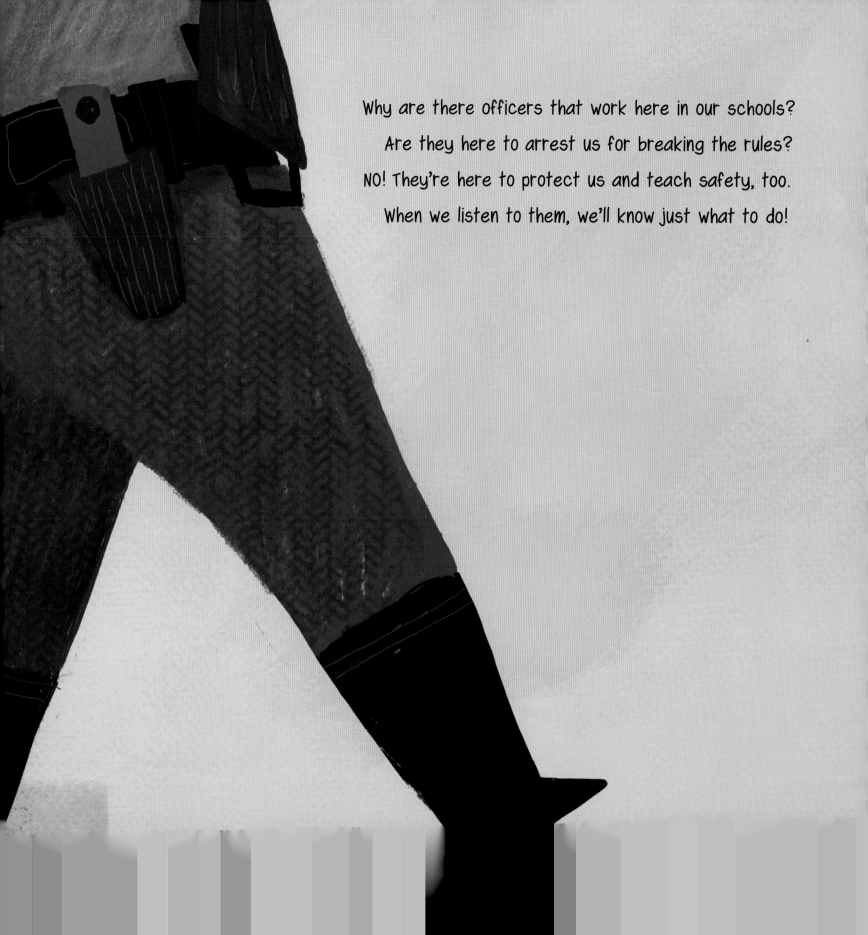

Why are there officers that work here in our schools?
Are they here to arrest us for breaking the rules?
NO! They're here to protect us and teach safety, too.
When we listen to them, we'll know just what to do!

On a regular school day, while Ben was in class,

someone new caught his eye in the door as they passed.

"Hey Katie! Look quick! I can't believe this at all!

I think a policewoman just walked down the hall!"

"I'm sure she's not a teacher; she had on BLACK SHOES
   and a BIG, HEAVY BELT like cops wear on the news!
And her shirt was LIGHT BROWN and her pants were DARK GREEN,
   that's not like any school teacher that I've ever seen."

LIGHT BROWN

"My dad said that police will sometimes dress in blue,

or in green, or in red, sometimes even brown, too!

And I did not see a badge, a shield, or a star.

But I'm sure that she came here in that awesome car!"

Then at once they ALL saw her, and there was NO doubt!

She said, "Hi!" and she waved...and then Ben just freaked out!

"Officers in our school with a badge and a gun?

Someone must be in trouble! We all need to run!

I thought you only saw them at scary events

like big fires, or big fights, or big car accidents!"

"Could it be?" Ben whispered. "Is it worse than I thought?

Is she here to get me? Have I finally been caught?

I shot Sam with a spit wad; filled Jill's pants with glue.

I tied Jack's shoes together—in triple knots, too!"

"Or is she here for Ms. Dean? I hope that is right!"

She teaches school by day and robs classrooms by night!

Is Ms. Dean a craft bandit when we turn our heads?

Stealing paper and crayons while we're in our beds!"

Then, Ms. Dean interrupted, "Kids, please all calm down.

That's our School Resource Officer walking around."

Sam leaned over to Ben, who was under a chair,

"She is not here for you Ben. Come on out of there!"

"The SRO is our friend, you don't need to hide.

In fact, we can all meet her. She's coming inside."

Some kids were quite excited, but others were scared.

When she walked in the classroom, they all stopped and stared.

"No one's in any trouble or under arrest.

And no, I cannot save you from your next math test!

I'm a deputy sheriff. I'll be here each day.

Here to help keep you safe while you learn and you play."

And then, Ben said to her, "Why, you seem pretty nice,
I think having you here will make bad guys think twice!
An SRO of our own protecting our school!
That's not scary at all, in fact...that's pretty cool!"

"See you tomorrow!"